Isaac and Rosa

All best wishes

The King of Kazam

For Kate, Finn, Lottie
and all other children who challenge
their parents when they're talking poo

All profits go to The Trussell Trust

The Trussell Trust supports a nationwide network of over 1,200 food banks, about two thirds of the food banks in the UK. These provided 2.5 million three-day emergency food supplies to people in crisis in 2020/21.

More than 14 million people in the UK live below the poverty line and struggle daily to feed themselves and their families. The Trussell Trust brings together the experiences of food banks, and their local communities, to help eradicate poverty and end the need for food banks in the UK.

The King of Kazam celebrates children who bravely challenge a King to share the riches of their kingdom with the whole community. The profit from every sale (£2) will be donated to The Trussell Trust via Work for Good.

www.trusselltrust.org
workforgood.co.uk

First published in Scotland in 2023 by Jen Hyatt Media

Text © Jen Hyatt
Illustration © Cassandra Harrison

The right of Jen Hyatt and Cassandra Harrison to be identified as the author and illustrator of this work has been asserted by them in accordance with the Copyright, Designs and Patents Act, 1998 (United Kingdom).

All rights reserved.

No part of this book may be reproduced, distributed or transmitted in any form or by any means, including photocopying, recording , or other electronic or mechanical methods, without the prior written permission of the publisher.

ISBN ISBN 978-1-7393751-0-2

Printed in the UK on paper sourced from FSC-certified suppliers

Designed by Helen Wyllie

The King of Kazam

Story by
Jen Hyatt

Illustrated by
Cassandra Harrison

The King of Kazam had a castle for life,
Two trendy kids, and a celebrity wife,
All of it run by a right royal team
Who kept ducks in a row and underwear clean.

'Team', said the King, 'while I may have it all,
I'm bored with royal visits and glittering balls.
I want something grand to mark out my reign,
Something amazing to carry my name.'

Each of the team avoided his gaze,
All were afraid of the King and his ways.
Even his children, Kandy and Kane
Wriggled in shame that their dad was so vain.

'Maybe a playground?' Kane asked the King.
'For all Kazam's kids', Kandy joined in.
They took out some chalks. They knew how to draw.
'Here let us show you.' They sketched on the floor,

Incredible slides snaking down from blue skies,
Swings hanging from rainbows and unicorn rides.
The King watched them draw; his eyes were alight.
He turned to his team, who were shaking with fright.

'My children are right. I have a great plan.
We'll build tributes to me, the King of Kazam!
Not nonsense for kids, or homes for sad losers,
But splendiferous palaces to honour your ruler!'

The right royal team trembled with shock,
They unsettled the ducks, mixed pants with the socks.

Kazam's kids were upset, as were Kandy and Kane.
Who whispered to others. 'Our dad's a right pain.
He always says 'No!' to slides, rides, and swings.
It's time we took action, let's trick the King.'

They ran to the top of a very tall hill,
They marked out a site and they started to build.

As Kandy and Kane made long curving slides,
Bright coloured swings and unicorn rides,
The King ordered grown-ups to work on his plan
Building castles galore for HM Kazam.

'Use lots of jewels and gold decorations.
What do I care about adding foundations,
If hammers are missing, and maybe some drills,
Or that all of the children are spoiling my hill?'

The right royal team were kept busy all day.
The ducks were unfed, the underwear grey.

The King kept on building, his money ran out,
'I cannot stop now, or let myself doubt.
I'm such a great ruler, I need so much more,
Constructions far greater than any before.

A shocking pink palace and one of sky-blue,
One floating on air and one made of bamboo.
He turned to his team. 'Calm down, just relax!
I'll pay for them all with another huge tax.'

'A tax, what's a tax?' asked Kandy and Kane.
'It's what people pay me,' their father explained.
'For houses and jobs, for all that they buy.
For living and working, and what's left when they die.
That's all there is to it, that's all that it means.
Taxes keep us in riches and cheer up the Queen.'

The right royal team weren't sure what to tax.
The ducks were all starving, the underwear slack.

There were taxes on dogs, on rats, cats and mice,
On bread, jam and honey, on brown and white rice.
There were taxes on winning and on losing too,
But there was no tax yet on flushing the loo.

'Right', said the King, 'To avoid money trouble,
A pee costs a pound, a poo costs you double.'
Each time you flush, the contents are tracked
By the right royal team who add up your tax.'

The King's brand new tax meant his palaces grew.
Though his subjects were cross, and cross-legged too
As they tried to hold in their pee and their poo,
To avoid paying tax when flushing the loo.

The right royal team were feeling the strain,
The ducks were revolting, the pants covered in stains.
Imagine counting every pee and each poo
And doing the maths on what taxes were due.

Kandy and Kane said, 'This isn't funny.
Our dad is greedy, he wants too much money.
And everyone's green trying to hold in their poo,
And no longer peeing or flushing the loo.'

IN 3 NEW SUPER TASTY CHOCOLATEY FLAVOURS

Choco Olives
Choco Prunes
Choco Turnips

For when you need to go but can't

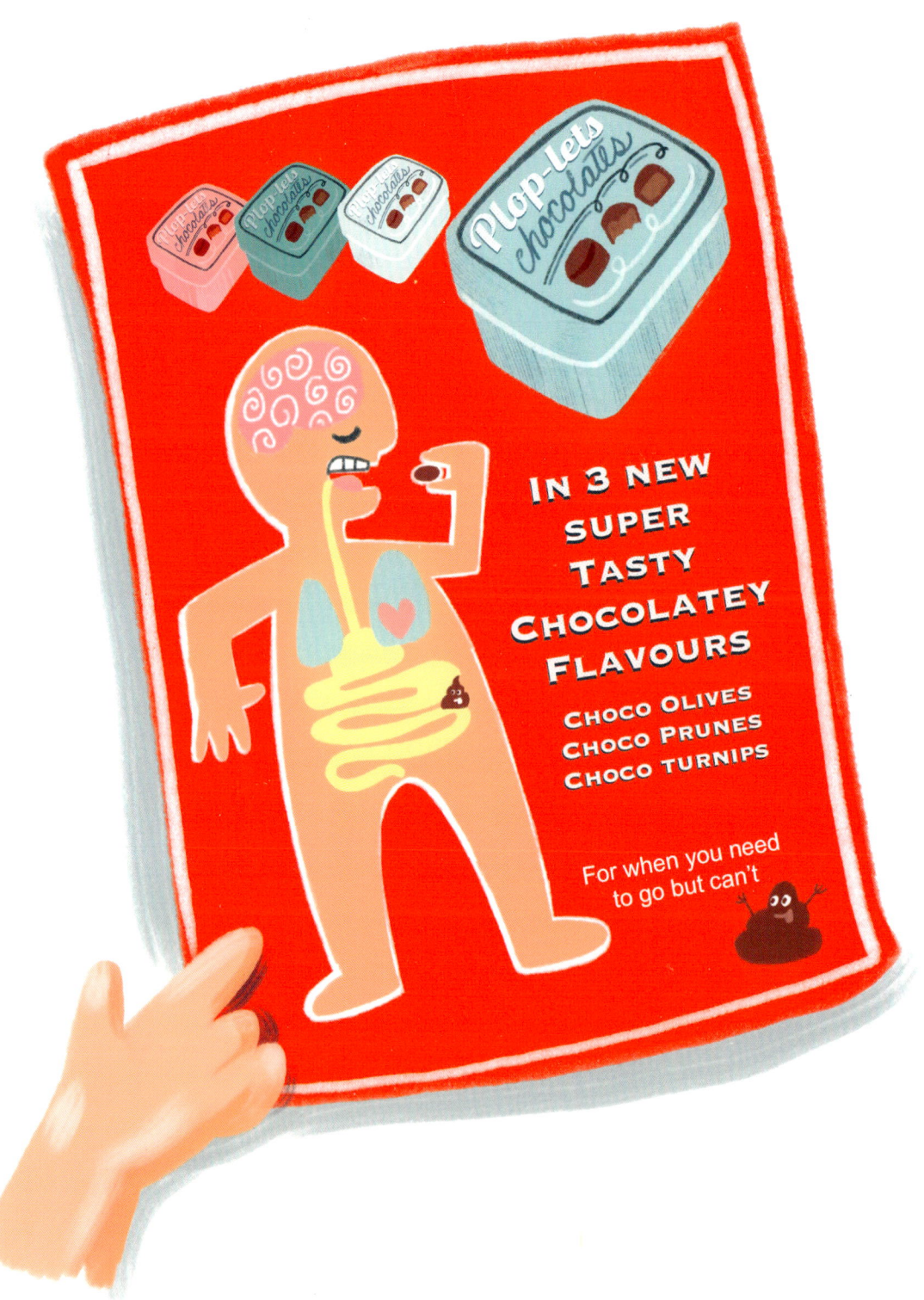

They gathered the kids to plan what to do.
To bring down the King and let people poo.
'When the King cannot poo after big feasts,
He eats some weird chocolate to help it release.

Feed this to your parents, it has a nice taste,
After they eat, it's not long to wait.
They'll dash to the toilet, not risking the chance
Of a moment's delay and a poop in their pants.

The right royal team thought the kingdom smelled rank.
The ducks had no feathers, the underwear stank.

All through Kazam, kids gave parents to eat
Lots of Plop Chocs, a nice tasting treat.
Soon grown-ups groaned, their fat tummies gurgled,
Went flipperty flopperty, babbled and burbled.

With panicked faces, they dashed to the loo.
And soon every toilet was full up of poo,
But due to the tax, no one dared flush,
The cost was too great, the money too much.

Poo sank through their floors
And burst open their doors.
It overflowed drains and ran down the streets
Picking up pace and covering feet.

When it rose above knees and up to their tums,
The townspeople yelled 'Up the hill! Quickly! Run!'
The King wouldn't go, nor his celebrity wife.
'We can't leave behind our rich royal life!'

The poo swelled and it slopped, it tipped over the top,
Then poured through the kingdom unable to stop.
It knocked down all palaces lacking foundations
It took the King and his wife, and their gold decorations.

Not a sound of regret was heard in the land.
No God Save the King! No 'I'll miss old Kazam'!

Kandy and Kane, on the hill way up high
Watched the right royal team wave a cheery goodbye
As the river of poo, took the King and his wife
Away from the kingdom and out of their sight.
They set the ducks free, made flags from the pants
Then ended all tax and did a victory dance.

Kandy and Kane had no wish to rule,
'Our dad was too greedy, a selfish old fool.
We realise his reign was incredibly tough
One King was too many and yet not enough.
What kind of man puts a tax on the loo,
Charging his people to pee and to poo.

Now all can go freely, enjoy every day,
Watch the ducks fly, see the kids play.
Zooming down slides that snake from blue skies,
Swinging from rainbows, taking unicorn rides.